Cats are such amazing animals!
They are very intelligent and have been associated with us, humans for over 9,500 years!

Fill with colors all cats in the book and read on for some cool facts about them so you're in the know!

A word for parents.

Thank you so much for trusting us with this coloring book. Introducing kids to pets in coloring books is a useful and important way to teach them to respect animals. Starting out with some interesting and cool cat facts can spark a lifetime of curiosity and care for felines.

Coloring books like this one are perfect not only for education and fun. They are a great help in stress relief, reducing anxiety, and developing imagination. Not mentioning a little peaceful moment for parents for a cup of coffee:) We hope your child will find it interesting! If so, we have more books from this series on Amazon.

If you consider rating the book on Amazon, it will mean a lot for our family self-publishing studio!

Wishing all the best,
Colorful Adventures Family Press.

The average cat sleeps 16 to 18 hours per day.

Cats can run up to
30 miles per hour.

Unlike humans, cats only sweat through their paws. This is why you may see them leave moist paw prints in the summer time!.

Cats can make more than 100 different vocal sounds.

An adult cat has
30 adult teeth.

A cat can jump approximately seven times their height.

Cats cannot taste
anything sweet.

A cat's sense of smell is approximately 14 times greater than that of a human.

A group of kittens is called a kindle; a group of adult cats is called a clowder.

Cats have five toes on each front paw, but only four toes on each back paw. Some cats have extra toes and are called "polydactyl" cats.

Cats who fall five stories have a 90 percent survival rate.

A cat's whiskers aren't just for show--they help cats detect objects and navigate in the dark.

A female cat carries her kittens for about 58 to 65 days before they are born.

Cats cannot see in complete darkness, only at low light levels.

Humans greet each other by shaking hands; cats greet one another by touching their noses together.

Cats can get tapeworm from eating mice.

Most cats are lactose intolerant and should not be given cow's milk.

Cats knead with their paws when they are happy.

Cats have sandpaper-like tongues that they use to clean and groom themselves.

Cats have sandpaper-like tongues that they use to clean and groom themselves.

Made in the USA
Monee, IL
09 June 2021